LILLE

DRAMA

Easter
PROGRAM
BUILDER
No.35

Creative Resources for
Program Directors

COMPILED BY HEIDI PETAK

lillenas

PUBLISHING COMPANY

Kansas City, MO 64141

Questions? Please write or call:
  Lillenas Publishing Company
  Drama Resources
  P. O. Box 419527
  Kansas City, MO 64141
  Phone: 816-931-1900 • Fax: 816-412-8390
  E-mail: drama@lillenas.com
  Website: www.lillenasdrama.com

Executive Editor: Heidi Petak
Supervising Editor: Kimberly Meiste
Copy Editor: Rachel Rummell
Manuscript Formatting: Karen Phillips
Cover Design by Sharon Page

Contents

Recitations for Children   5

Adult Readings and Recitations   7

Sketches   15

    Shattered Dreams   15

    Our Crucified Lord   20

    Conversation Between Two Intellectuals   21

Palm Sunday / Easter Service Ideas   24

    Easter Reading for Two   24

    They Knew No Easter   26

    Called by Name   35

Recitations for Children

Big Praise for Little Hearts

My little hands can clap, clap, clap;
My little voice can sing,
My little heart believes it's true,
That Jesus is my King!

by Heidi Petak

Clap, Clap

Clap, clap, clap your hands,
Shout aloud,
And with us dance.
Lift, lift, lift your voice,
Sing your praise,
With us rejoice.

by L. Ruth Carter

Easter Love

ADULT: We love lots of things
about Easter, like . . .

CHILD 1: Candy!

CHILD 2: Finding eggs!

CHILD 3: Easter baskets!

CHILD 4: Chocolate bunnies!

ADULT: I love all those things too.
But who do we love most?

ALL CHILDREN: Jesus!

ADULT: Why?

ALL CHILDREN: Because He is alive!
(CHILDREN cheer.)

by Heidi Petak

A Baby, A Savior

Who could have known a baby
Born in Bethlehem's stall,
Could possibly be the Messiah,
Born to save us all?

by Carolyn R. Scheidies

Surprise at the Tomb

*(May be performed by one child, a group
of children, or split between six children.
ALL children would say the last line
together in unison.)*

The first day I went to Jesus' tomb.
(Hold up one finger)

The stone had sealed it tight.
(Put right fist into left palm)

The second day I went to Jesus'
tomb. *(Hold up two fingers)*

I pushed that stone with all my
might. *(Push with both hands)*

(Big sigh)

The third day I went to Jesus' tomb.
(Hold up three fingers)

The stone is gone! What a sight!
*(Both hands out to sides, elbows
bent, palms up)*

Jesus is alive! *(Children cheer)*

by Heidi Petak

The Little Donkey

We had a little donkey
just as sweet as he can be.
I liked to give him hay to eat.
He liked to nuzzle me.

I asked if I could ride him,
but my father shook his head.
He said, "This donkey's special,"
and then sent me off to bed!

One day some men untied him.
They said, "It's for the Master."
And then I saw the crowds begin
to move faster and faster.

I heard the people calling,
"It's Jesus. Come and see!"
And then I ran right with them.
My father ran with me!

The crowd called out, "Hosanna!
Hosanna, David's Son!"
Someone said, "It's Jesus!
But what's He riding on?"

And then we saw our donkey,
so proud and sweet and strong
And Jesus sat right on him
just smiling at the throng.

"I knew that he was special,"
my dad said with a sigh.
I think our donkey winked at me
as he carried Jesus by!
                    by Beth Swale

Not the Manger

We bow at the manger
As joy fills our hearts
That Christ would come as a baby,
But Christmas is just the start . . .

We tell the Savior's story,
The Savior who gave up everything
To walk the earth as God-man,
Salvation and new life to bring.

For Jesus came to save us,
Took our place at Calvary,
Rose to offer hope and life
Now and for eternity.

So on this Easter morning
We bow not before a baby,
But the risen Christ who died, yet
lives
That we might be
In Him,
Wholly and completely *free*.
                    by Carolyn R. Scheidies

No More Sad Good-byes

My grandpa died not long ago.
He was my favorite friend.
I didn't want to say good-bye
As if it was the end.

And so I said, "I'll see you soon,"
Because I know it's true.
My grandpa is alive and well
And his body is all new.

I still cry but I can't wait
To see Grandpa with my eyes.
The Easter promise is my hope
For no more sad good-byes.

The grave now has no victory
And death has lost its sting
Because my Jesus rose again
And is my Living King.
                    by Heidi Petak

Adult Readings & Recitations

No Easter

by Jill Orr

Running Time: 5 minutes

Cast:
READER 1
READER 2
READER 3
READER 4

Props:
Crown of thorns
Dove
Easter lily
Robe

Setting: A simple backdrop of a cross

ALL: Easter is . . .

READER 1: A time of new beginnings when the past can be put behind us. The chains that were forged from past sins, mistakes, and bad choices have held us prisoner. Now the chains are broken. They fall in the dust and we move forward to the future, rubbing our wrists in disbelief.

READER 2: A time for resurrection, where life is born again. The dreams that were shattered take root and are given new life. Our dreams grow, taking on a new dimension that was shaped by trials and tribulations.

READER 3: A time for hope. With God all things are possible.

ALL: Easter is . . .

READER 4: A time of redemption, when we are restored to wholeness through God's love and mercy. He takes our broken pieces and mends them, molding us into the creatures He wants us to be.

READER 1: A time of unconditional love. God poured out His love for the world in the most unique and unexpected way. He loved us so much that He gave everything He was and risked everything for you and me.

READER 2: A time of forgiveness. God forgives each sin, each denial, each betrayal.

ALL: Easter is . . .

READER 3: A time of faith. A time to believe in our Risen Lord and King and trust in Him.

READER 4: A time of truth. Lies can no longer survive. Darkness is swallowed up by light.

READER 1: A time of peace and rest. We can release all our burdens to Jesus and rest in His arms.

READER 2: A time of healing, for "by his stripes we are healed."

READER 3: A time of victory and celebration. Death is defeated. Our Lord and Savior reigns. Without the miracle of Easter and God's love, there would be . . .

(During this segment the cross and props are stripped away until the space is empty and bare.)

READER 1: No release. We would always be held prisoner by our past, never free to walk away from it and begin anew.

READER 2: No spring borne out of winter's laboring pains. No bright colors. Only washed out gray, black, and white. *(Remove lily)*

READER 3: No rebirth or new beginnings. There would only be dead ends and one-way streets from which there is no return.

READER 4: No hope. Fear and worry would be our constant companions. *(Remove dove)*

READER 1: No redemption. We would be drowning forever in our sins. *(Remove crown)*

READER 2: No love. There would be nothing to nurture us, to help us blossom and grow.

READER 3: Instead of forgiveness, there would be revenge and cruelty. *(Remove robe)*

READER 4: Doubt would prevent us from ever accomplishing anything or helping anyone.

READER 1: Lies and deceit would be rampant.
Turmoil would increase.
Disease and sickness would multiply with no cure in sight. *(Remove cross)*
Death would reign. There would be no life—only a meaningless existence.
Life would be empty and bare.
Can you imagine a world with no Easter?

(Voices echo the last two words: "No Easter.")

Loved Defined by a King

by Chris Baxter

(To be performed by a woman.)

I have been chosen to be the King's bride, of this great land?
How can this be?
Am I worthy of His hand?
No, my heart knows that I am not!
Nevertheless, He has declared His love, and sought
My beauty?
To think, He sings to me, and rejoices over me,
And then He quiets me—all with His love.
How can this be,
That He has chosen *me?*

Now, my eye is upon Him . . .

The great High King *is* strong and mighty,
Full of splendor and majesty.

His sword is at His thigh,
And I have seen Him ride—victoriously.
With His sharp arrows, He dashes evil to the ground.
So that, in His land, truth and meekness may abound.
He teaches awesome things—and all will profess,
His scepter stands for righteousness.
Oh, how my heart has fallen
As I watch the majesty of my King!
How beautiful You are to me,
My soul will forever sing.

Now yes, He does ride with strength and with might,
But it is in His gentleness that my heart takes delight.

He walks with me, and talks with me, and sweetly takes my hand.
He cares for me; He listens to me—
His love I try to understand!
 When He looks at me . . .
  I see in His eyes—acceptance,
  I feel in His love—security.

He says, "You are mine, my bride, and I am yours.
 I will never leave you, in this you can be sure.
 The mountains may tremble, and the hills may shake,
 But my love for you will never die.
 No, nothing will cause *this* love to separate—
  Neither height nor depth,
  Nor life nor death,
  No, *nothing* will pull me from your side.
 You are my chosen one; you are my lovely one.
 You are my sweet, precious bride."

Oh, how my heart trembles at His words,
And then, with an overwhelming shout,
I say, "My King, a day in Your courts is better than a thousand without.
 How I long to live with You forever,
 In this I do not doubt."
And I will always sing of this overwhelming theme:
"His banner over me is . . . love."

But soon, the King's greatest enemy was told.
And from a distance, he saw the love story unfold.
Because he was so full of hate—
He raged, "This Love I *cannot* tolerate!"
So in anger he began to oversee
A wretched plot, an evil scheme—
"I came to destroy *any good thing*," he demands.
"And I will rip this Love right from His hands!"

So, like a thief in the night, the enemy came.
I was captured, bound, and taken away.
He left me in a dark, lonely place—
And there, over time, my King's love seemed to fade.

Left alone, afraid, and in despair—
    "Will He find me? Does He care?
    Does He know? Was He even real?
    My King's love for me, now, I can hardly feel!
    Where are You, my love? Will You come?
    Oh please, oh *please*, save me from this evil one!"

Just as my confidence began to fully wane,
Of course the King had heard, and I was told, He came.
I was taken, still bound, to the top of a hill,
One that overlooked a plush, green field,
And there! In the distance my beloved King stood.
On His great white horse,
Oh, I knew no one could
Overcome my Love, so majestic and sweet.
My King had come to **fight** and to **defeat**!
    Yes, He had come
    And yes, He was real—
    I will watch Him ride,
    I will make my appeal:
        "Ride, O King
        Take him down . . .
            Set me free."

The black horse and his rider stood in place—
I could see nothing but evil on his face.
Only vengeance was in his eyes.
Then, he rode toward the King with his sword upright.
My King, too, began His mission.
But in His face—I saw love, I saw strength, I saw mercy, I saw compassion.
Yet, His focus did not settle with the evil coming on,
No, as He rode, He gazed at me—to whom His heart belonged!

My heart raced as the horses ran . . .

"Lift up Your sword," I whispered to my King.
"Slay the wicked, and kill every evil thing!
Lift up Your sword," I said again.
"You're a valiant warrior, and goodness is Your friend."
"Lift up Your sword," I proclaimed even louder.
"What are You doing? Don't You see he's coming closer?
Pick it up!" I shouted with a frightening plea . . .
"Didn't You come to fight for me?"

My mind a blur, my heart astir
I watched in disbelief.
"My King! My King! It is Your life for mine?
No! In this, there will be endless grief!"
Yet, with His head tilted back and His arms stretched out wide,
He never reached for the sword at His side.
Instead, more gently and humbly than any other man,
He steadfastly continued to hold out His hands.

And in an instant that seemed like forever,
    Good and evil clashed together.
    My heart could hardly take it all.
    My King was pierced,
    And I watched my Love fall.

"No!" I cried as I felt my chains loosen.
"No!" I yelled as I began to run to Him.
"No!" I wept as I met my Love where He had fallen.
I cradled His sweet head, holding onto His last breaths.

His eyes so sweet, His love so deep.
"What have You done? O my King?
I never asked You to die for me!"
I broke, I cried, as He willingly gave His life.

I listened, and He answered in a slow steady tone:
"What I did for you, my love, had to be done.
    Neither silver nor gold,
    Could break the hold,
    Of this evil one.
Now, go, get up, love, live on.
Please do not grieve any more over me—
For it is by my blood, my queen,
That you are *free*!"

And then He closed His eyes on life . . .

My heart sank, my soul died,
My mind went blank as they pulled Him from my side.
He told me to live on . . .
How can this be—when my whole life was just snatched from me?
And He told me to love . . .
This I cannot do—for all my love was just pierced through.
No, there was no going on for me.
I stayed there bent over, broken, and continued to weep.
No, there was no going on for me.
My world was gone, I was *not* free!
Family, friends, could not comfort, no, not anyone.
All I could see was that my life, too, was gone.
    "Please go away, please leave me alone—
    I have to weep, and I will never be strong!"

So I stayed and pushed all love away.

How long was I there, bent over my knees?
One minute? One hour? One day? Two? Or Three?

Time is lost in the mourning of Love . . .

Once more I heard footsteps come—
"No," I whispered, "please leave me alone."
They kept coming forward—steady, persistent.
But in these steps, *hope* was the difference.
A gentle hand, a familiar touch, sweetly, slowly lifted my chin.

Then, my eyes looked up, and my heart leapt within!
"What has happened?
How can this be?
How *could* this happen?
He's come back for me?
He has Risen!
Impossible, but beautiful,
Incredible, but true;
Yes, He has come again!
How can this be?
My life, my love, made new!"

He took my hand; He lifted me
From the pit of my despair.
He wiped the tears from my eyes,
And held me with tender care.

"Yes," I cried, "My Redeemer lives!
Yet what manner of love is this He gives?"

I looked in His eyes, He looked in mine.
And I remembered His words clearly ring:
"I will never leave you, My love—
And now, you know, in *My* death, there is no sting."

He walked with me, and talked with me
And told me amazing things—
I listened to Him, and learned from Him,
Oh—for my *mind* to see!

"You see, My bride," He began to confide . . .

"*I AM* more than King of this one land.
I AM King of kings
I AM Lord of lords.
I hold the universe in My hands.
I placed the sun; I hung the moon.
I named the stars, each one.
I AM righteousness
I AM holiness
I AM your Savior, Jesus Christ, God's Son.

But it is not by might, nor by power
But by My Spirit I have come . . .
To make you, mold you, move you
Into My arms of Love.
Here I will hold you, protect you, keep you—
And then, *live inside your heart* forever!
Will you allow Me to abide with you?
For it would be My honor and My pleasure."

Once again I went to my knees
But now giving reverence to Whom it was due.
I could not decipher if I was more awed

By Who He was,
Or because it was *me* that His love pursued!

"O Lord, God, Creator, King
Yes, I believe in You.
But that You, sweet Jesus,
Love *me* this way?
Oh help me in my unbelief!"
"How could it be that I should gain
    The love of this King of Glory?
Who am I to deserve such love,
    Oh, what a beautiful story!
        His love is long
        His love is wide
    It is high, and it is deep.
To think that His love was meant for me,
How precious, and so, so sweet."

So I trusted Him, His love for me,
And we walked along together
Again, He told me of incredible things,
Then He vowed His love to me . . . *forever.*

Bend and Break This Bough

by J. Bernadette Williamson

Oh Sacred Vine of Calvary,
This branch entwines her heart to You.
So ever grafted we shall be,
Sting to sting—Wound to wound.

Come wash my garments in the wine
Pressed from the grapes of Passion's
tree.
Whisper, I'm forever Thine,
So intimate the agony.

Oh priceless gift from pierced hands;
Precious sight from sorrow wrought.
Spilling the fragrance of Your blood
Like perfume down a rugged cross.

You've drawn me to Your bleeding side,
Hung my fists on jagged nails,
Breathed surrender's breath in me,
Shared the air of sweet travail.

I've tasted many other loves
But savored none so fiercely pure.
The satin upon Your spotless brow
Leaves my soul but thirstier.

"Come drink" . . . You murmur in the
rage.
Thus I commune and am assuaged.
'Tis in the bitter cup of grief
The quench of joy rejuvenates.

Lord, crush my pride by holy measure.
Sever 'til the suffering
Yields abundance for Your pleasure,
Brings a harvest flourishing.

I will be forever Yours.
You will be forever mine.
I am Your devoted branch.
You are my Beloved Vine.

Bend and break this bough.
Cut the cords of vanity.
Bend and break me now
'Til there's nothing left of me.

Bend and break this bough,
Recklessly Your will to do.
Bend and break me now
'Til there's nothing left but You.

Jesus Came

by Carolyn R. Scheidies

Running Time: 4 to 7 minutes

Cast: 1 to 5 individuals/groups

Production Note: All individuals/groups should recite the last verse *(John 14:19 is read aloud by one individual. Script continues.)*

Jesus
Came to earth a baby,
Lived a life like you and me.
A baby,
A child,
A man.

Yet more . . .
He was Savior,
Lord of all,
Following God's master plan.

He cared,
Was there,
Healed the sick by His own hand.

Died and rose again that
You and I
Would be free
As we
Come to Him.

Confess our sin,
Accept new life within,
Completely,
Abundantly,
Eternally.

We bow in gratitude and worship
On this Easter Day.
Honoring Christ who leads us
To truth, to life, to the Way.

(John 3:16-17 is read aloud. Conclude with the song "Amazing Grace.")

Sketches

Shattered Dreams

by Andrea P. Johnson

Running Time: 15 to 20 minutes

Synopsis: An interview with Mary, Jesus' mother, gives us insight into Jesus' life, crucifixion, and resurrection from a mother's point of view. In addition to giving people the opportunity to reflect on Jesus' life, it also shows us that God's ways are beyond our understanding. Disappointments don't necessarily mean we have failed, nor do they mean God has failed. Instead, they show that God has something different—usually much better—in mind.

Cast:

HOST

MARY—Mother of Jesus

Props:

Slides with pictures from Jesus' life, if available

or

Photo album for host and guest to look through

Costumes: Period robe and headdress for Mary; suit outfit for host

(Television studio, interview setup)

HOST *(addressing the audience):* Welcome to our show, *Dreaming Big.* Have you ever had a dream you felt sure was from God? You know, one of those times when you were certain God was leading you . . . but after several attempts at pursuing that dream, you began to wonder if you had heard from God at all?

    Today, I am going to introduce you to a special guest, an extraordinary lady who had her share of shattered dreams, but managed to keep the faith through it all. Ladies and gentlemen, please welcome Mary, the mother of Jesus!

(MARY enters the room. The two greet each other and both sit down.)

Picture: Angel and Mary

HOST: Mary, thank you so much for taking time out to visit with us today. We are talking about shattered dreams. You have certainly experienced your share, so I'm going to ask you some questions and maybe we can glean some insight from your experiences. Let's start at the beginning of your adventure. As we see in this picture, the angel Gabriel has come to you and announced that you were going to give birth to the Messiah, to Jesus. How did you respond?

MARY: Well, I was shocked, to say the least. Though I was a descendant of David, my family was poor. I was humbled and honored at the same time . . . Nearly every woman in Israel hoped to hear the news I had just heard, that my child would be the Messiah. Yet . . . I was pledged to be married to Joseph. I had dreams of the "white wedding dress. " What would Joseph think when I told him I was expecting a child? What would my family and others think? Would they believe me when I tried to explain that I was still a virgin?

HOST: That would be awkward. How did Joseph react?

MARY: I'll never forget the look in his eyes when I told him . . . a mixture of disbelief, disappointment, and hurt. Joseph was a good man though. He could have had me stoned. Thankfully, the Lord appeared to him in a dream and told him not to be afraid to take me as his wife. I was "with child" through the Holy Spirit. At times I wished the others would have had that dream. Few people believed me. I mean, would you? Many thought Joseph was crazy for sticking by me.

HOST: You must have felt so alone.

MARY: You have no idea . . . Thankfully, Gabriel told me that my cousin Elizabeth was also with child. Can you imagine? In her old age? I just had to go see her. I thought maybe she would help me make sense of everything.

Picture: Mary greeting Elizabeth

What a difference that visit made! As soon as Elizabeth saw me, she cried out, "Blessed are you among women, and blessed is the child you will bear!" She knew my baby was her future Lord. In fact, her baby recognized it as well, and literally leapt in her womb! Those days brought me the reassurance I needed for the next part of my journey.

HOST: Yes, the next part of your journey must have been rough as well. You would think that God would have had a different plan for the birth of His Son.

Picture: Mary and Joseph on their journey

I mean, really, bouncing up and down on the back of a donkey for 70 long miles near the end of your pregnancy? No wonder you went into labor! And a manger? You had to put the Son of God in a manger!

MARY: Oh, I know. God's ways are not our ways, that's for sure. One would have thought a descendent of King David, God's Son, would have been born amongst princes and royalty. Instead, Israel's future King was born among common stable animals.

Picture: Manger scene

HOST: And yet, even though it was in a stable, you still gave birth. Describe your feelings when you saw your son for the first time?

Picture: Mary and Jesus

MARY: I can hardly talk about it without tears. Birth is such a miracle. To think, this beautiful baby boy had been in my womb just moments before. I counted His tiny little toes and fingers, kissed His perfect little button nose, and gazed into His gorgeous eyes. I've never felt love like that before. As He snuggled against me, I realized the absurdity and beauty of it all. The future Savior of the world was dependent on me for nourishment. He was so vulnerable.

16

And yet it was exciting. The visits of the wise men, the shepherds, Simeon and Anna in the Temple . . . all of them confirmed that our child was indeed the salvation of mankind! Joseph and I were humbled, amazed, ecstatic, and sobered. God had entrusted this little guy to us!

HOST: I can't imagine the weight of that responsibility . . . which brings us to the infamous Temple visit when you lost Jesus. Tell me, what happened there?

Picture: Jesus in the Temple

MARY *(chuckles):* You would bring that up. Well, when Jesus was twelve, as was our custom, we traveled to Jerusalem for the Feast of the Passover. On these trips we would go in caravans, for safety's sake. The women and children would travel in front, and the men in back. I thought Jesus was with Joseph, and Joseph thought He was with me. When we finally realized Jesus was not with either group, we returned to Jerusalem to find Him. After three days I was starting to panic.

HOST *(interrupts):* Oh my goodness. Now, whenever I'm in trouble the first thing I do is to pray. Just how do you pray in a situation like that? I mean, what do you say, *(sheepishly)* "Excuse me, Lord, but I've . . . ummm . . . I've lost Your Son . . .?"

MARY *(chuckles):* Something like that . . . Finally, we found Jesus at the Temple among the teachers, debating with them—on their level. They were amazed at His understanding. I said, "Jesus, don't You know how worried Your father and I have been trying to find You?" He just looked at me and said, "Wouldn't you know that I would be in my Father's house?" I realized then that we had gone into the Temple looking for our little boy, but what we found was a young man eager to get on with His Father's plans for His life.

HOST: Your little boy was growing up. And then, we don't really hear anything about Jesus for the next 18 years. What happened during those years?

MARY: Those were what we call our "normal" years. Jesus came of age, just like any other young man. He grew physically and mentally. As the oldest child in a large family, He carried a great deal of responsibility. But mostly we were just normal people living normal lives. I doubt Jesus thought it was very exciting.

HOST: And then, when Jesus turned 30, all that changed.

MARY: It sure did.

Picture: Jesus teaching, healing, etc.

For three years, my son—God's Son—spent every waking moment serving others; healing, teaching, performing miracles, casting out demons, calming violent storms—literally . . . He even walked on water! Huge crowds followed Him. He had to sneak away just to find time to talk alone with His Heavenly Father. And when He did escape from the crowds, His disciples were always there, asking questions, fighting for His attention. I rarely got to see Him.

HOST: And then, in one week's time, Jesus went from rock star status, to being nailed on the cross.

Picture: Palm Sunday entry into Jerusalem

HOST: What happened?

Picture: Arrest

MARY: Oh, you know, the usual—politics . . . envy . . . greed . . . you name it. Jesus had such a large following, our leaders were afraid He would overthrow them. I found out they had Him arrested in the middle of the night and tortured Him.

Picture: Trial and beating

> The trial . . . it was such a farce. The Jewish leaders, the Roman politicians, the soldiers . . . such weak individuals. No one stood up for my son. He could have annihilated them without blinking, yet He took it all.

HOST: Their treatment of Him, it seems excessive for a political crime.

MARY: It was pure evil. You would have thought He was some mass murderer. And yet, He had never laid a hand on anyone, except to heal them.

HOST: What about all those people, the ones He had healed . . . and the disciples, surely they stood up for Him when Jesus was arrested?

MARY: Oh no, they all fled, even Peter, who had just earlier in the night pledged, "Even if I have to die with you, I will never disown you!" When He needed friends the most, my son was alone.

HOST *(pauses, knowing this will be a difficult question):* And the next time you saw Him?

MARY: It's hard for me to talk about, but it must be told. *(Pauses, looks away, and takes a deep breath, as if steeling herself.)*

Picture: Via Dolorosa

> I had heard about Jesus' arrest, so several of us, mostly women, tried to find Him. We met up with Him just as they were leading Him away—to be crucified. *(Gives a little sob)* I didn't even recognize my own son; He had been beaten so badly. They tried to make Him carry His own cross but He was so weak from the torture, He stumbled. Like blood-thirsty wolves, they yanked Him up and forced Him to march on. They made another man, Simon, carry the cross. The whole time they were mocking Jesus and beating Him. They spit on Him. My friends and I, we couldn't believe this was really happening.

HOST: I'm so sorry. And when they got to Golgotha?

MARY: When they got to Golgotha, Calvary, they threw the cross on the ground. Then they threw my Jesus on top of that cross and they nailed His hands to it.

Picture: Jesus being nailed to the cross

> Those hands . . . those hands that had built tables and cradles, even houses . . . those hands that healed the blind and the lame and the insane . . . those same hands that had once held mine . . . those precious hands were nailed to a cross.

> *(Sobbing)* The actual crucifixion, well, I'm sorry. I can't talk about it.

HOST: It must have been agonizing. And there's no need to go into detail. But what were you thinking when they raised that cross in the air?

Picture: Jesus on the cross

MARY: I thought, "Where was God? Why didn't He stop this horrible nightmare? Why didn't Jesus stop it? He had saved the others. Why wouldn't He save himself? Had I done something wrong? Had I failed? Had God? Why was this happening?" *(Breaks down, weeping)*

HOST *(gently):* So after all the promises . . . the prophecies . . . Jesus died on that cross. You must have felt like all was lost.

MARY *(through tears):* All was lost. My son was dead. God's plan had failed—or so I thought. But . . . early in the morning on the third day, I went to Jesus' tomb with some friends to anoint Jesus' body with spices. We were asking on the way there how we were ever going to move that huge stone from the mouth of the tomb. But when we got there, the stone had already been rolled away!

HOST: How do you explain that?

MARY: A supernatural miracle. That stone must have weighed a thousand pounds! And then these men in dazzling white garments—angels, we think—told us that Jesus had risen from the dead! We ran as fast as we could back to the disciples to tell them the good news. And then, a few days later, when we were all gathered together, Jesus suddenly appeared in the midst of us! I saw Him with my own eyes! I know now that the cross was not the end. Death could not hold God's Son. And what I had thought was the end was just the beginning.

HOST: Mary, what a great story! Thank you so much for sharing it with us. As you know, there are people in the audience today who have experienced shattered dreams as well. What would you say to them?

MARY: Oh, I would say to keep trusting in God, and never give up hope. He doesn't break His promises. If He gave you a dream, He will make it happen—in better ways than you can ever imagine.

HOST: Thank you, Mary, for being my guest today. All the best to you. And to you, our viewing audience, until next time, keep *Dreaming Big*.

Our Crucified Lord

by Dorothy Heibel

Running Time: 5 minutes

Cast:

> PROCULA—Wife of Pontius Pilate
>
> LIVIA—Procula's maid servant

(Living quarters of Pointius Pilate and PROCULA *in Jerusalem; late morning;* PROCULA *is seated on bench.* LIVIA *enters.)*

PROCULA: Ah, Livia, is it really morning?

LIVIA: Yes, my lady. Did you not sleep well?

PROCULA: No. It is this way every time the Passover takes place in Jerusalem. There are crowds of people and clouds of dust everywhere!

LIVIA: The Passover seems to be of great importance to the Jewish people.

PROCULA: And every year my husband, Pontius Pilate, comes to Jerusalem to keep order. The Jewish leaders are so loud and demanding! These men who consider themselves so righteous are condemning an innocent man to death.

LIVIA: An innocent man? But is it not criminals who are put to death, criminals whose lives are not valuable . . . thieves and robbers . . . every year this takes place at the Passover . . .

PROCULA: But this man is not a thief or a robber. He is quite different.

LIVIA: What do you mean, my lady?

PROCULA: This man they call Jesus can cure the crippled and cause the blind to see!

LIVIA: Perhaps He is an imposter who pretends to be a great healer!

PROCULA: No, no. There was a man who had been a cripple for years! His friends brought him to Jesus on a stretcher. The man was sure Jesus could cure him. Jesus only said, "Take up your bed and walk," and the man did. Jesus also brought a dead man back to life again . . . a man named Lazarus.

LIVIA: You could not change the mind of Pontius Pilate, then?

PROCULA *(wringing her hands):* You can see I tried, but to no avail. My husband does not wish to offend the Jewish leaders. He is afraid it would start a riot if he would free Jesus. Oh, Livia, he has delivered an innocent man into their hands.

LIVIA: Then, my lady, there is nothing more you can do! What will be, will be. And once you are back in Rome, this will all be forgotten!

PROCULA: If only I could have made my husband understand. Oh, listen to the noise in the street . . . the shouting . . .

(Several voices from offstage: "Crucify Him! Crucify Him!" PORCULA *may also say these words.)*

LIVIA: How odd! The sun has left the portals. It is growing dark and it is still only mid-day! Oh no, I can feel the earth trembling!

PROCULA: Oh, Livia, we are being punished for taking the life of an innocent man, a holy man. Oh God, have mercy on Pontius Pilate! God, have mercy on us!

Conversation Between Two Intellectuals

by Thomas Golden

Running Time: 10 to 15 minutes

Cast:

Dr. Roy Aloysius Bean

Dr. Jacob Mellowman

(Lights up on two intellectuals in two chairs.)

ROY: Good morning and welcome to *A Conversation between Two Intellectuals on the Nature of Reaching out to a Largely Un-Churched Nation*. I am your host, Dr. Roy Aloysius Bean. My guest today is Dr. Jacob Mellowman, professor emeritus at the University of Bobby Davis in Deport, Texas, and author of the book *Fascism: Would God Have Minded So Much?* Today's topic: "To picket or not to picket," and "Love thy neighbor, or beat thy neighbor into submission." Dr. Mellowman, I will let you start us out.

JACOB: Roy, if the crusades taught us one thing it was very clear that the only way to effectively reach an un-churched nation is by the sheer brute force that God endowed His people with from the beginning: The tools of missions and conversion.

ROY: Which would be?

JACOB: Nucular warheads. Nothing truly says "Love my God" as the threat of all out nucular war.

ROY: My dear Dr. Mellowman, I am afraid you have made a terrible mistake.

JACOB: Have I?

ROY: Yes, you see the word is pronounced Nuclear. Not Nuc*u*lar.

JACOB: Did I say nuc*u*lar?

ROY: I'm afraid you did, old man.

JACOB: Dear me. How embarrassing.

ROY: Quite all right, my friend. What kind of a Christian would I be if I didn't forgive your faux pas. *(Pronounced "foh-pah")*

JACOB: Thanks, old man.

ROY: Don't mention it.

JACOB: But I have.

ROY: So you have. Please continue, Doctor.

JACOB: Now the most important thing that we must force through on the heathen brood is the resurrection of Christ. I cannot make this any clearer. Even if you have to beat the truth of the resurrection into the un-churched, the effort will be well worth the energy.

ROY: I must agree. So many times non-believers will tell the story of Christ and stop at the crucifixion. They crucify Him all day long but never resurrect Him. Do you think there is a reason for this?

JACOB: A lack of proper attention span, I suppose.

ROY: But how does one lose attention when recounting such a thing?

JACOB: Well, I don't claim to be an expert on the psyche of the modern audience, but when we made "The Great Film" . . .

ROY: You were there for "The Great Film?"

JACOB: Wasn't it amazing? Changed my life.

ROY: Oh, changed many lives.

JACOB: Too many to count.

ROY: Too true. I would be wont to determine the exact number of the multitude who were changed by this film alone.

JACOB: Now . . . where was I . . . what were we talking about?

ROY: Eh . . .

JACOB: Uh . . .

ROY: Attention spans!

JACOB: Ah yes, attention spans. Nasty little buggers.

ROY: Attention spans.

JACOB: What about them then?

ROY: They . . . they aren't long enough.

JACOB: Far too short.

ROY: Entirely too short.

JACOB: Too short for what?

ROY: Oh . . . crucifixion. They are too short for the whole story of the crucifixion.

JACOB: Oh wonderful story, the crucifixion. The ultimate sacrifice to heal a wounded world.

(As they discuss this the tension and excitement builds to a great crescendo.)

ROY: The triumphant entry!

JACOB: Last supper!

ROY: Betrayal!

JACOB: The trial!

ROY: The denial!

JACOB: The second denial!

ROY: The third!

JACOB: Cock-a-doodle-doo!

ROY: The Via Dolorosa!

JACOB: Riots!

ROY: The abuse!

JACOB: The pain!

ROY: The love!

JACOB: The spilling of sinless blood!

ROY: The righting of all wrongs!

JACOB: Nails!

ROY: Death!

(They are both now standing and shouting. This is the climax.)

BOTH: It is finished!

(They come down from their excitement and take their seats.)

ROY: Are we missing anything?

JACOB: I don't think so.

ROY: Good, well, happy Easter.

JACOB: Happy Easter.

(They exit in different directions. Blackout.)

Palm Sunday / Easter Service Ideas

Easter Reading for Two

by Beth Westcott

Running Time: 30 minutes

Scripture References: Isaiah 53:1-7; Psalm 22; Matthew 27, 28:1-7; Mark 16:1-7; Luke 24:1-10; 1 John 1:1-3; Galatians 4:4-7

Cast:

> READER 1
>
> READER 2

READER 1: At just the right time in history,

READER 2: in just the right place,

READERS 1 & 2: God sent His Son to earth,

READER 2: born of a human mother,

READER 1: to bring mankind redemption
from slavery to the law.

READER 2: Adopted by God as His children,
through His Spirit, we call Him "Abba—Father."

READER 1: No longer servants, but His children
and heirs with Jesus Christ.
(from Galatians 4:4-7)

Song: "He Is Lord" *(Refrain)*

READERS 1 & 2: Who will believe what God has revealed to us?

READER 2: He shall grow up as a tender plant out of dry ground.

READER 1: There is nothing about His physical appearance
that would make Him stand out in the crowd.
In fact, mankind despised and rejected Him.

READERS 1 & 2: We turned our faces away from Him
as He suffered great sorrow and grief.

READER 1: It was our grief and sorrow—

READER 2: our great burden of sin and its penalty—

READERS 1 & 2: that He bore for us.

READER 1: He was wounded in our place,

READER 2: hurt for our sins,

READER 1: so that through His suffering

READERS 1 & 2: we can be healed.

READER 2: We are all like straying sheep;
instead of following the Shepherd
we decided to each take our own path.

READER 1: He suffered for our disobedience.
But though He suffered so greatly,
He never complained.

READERS 1 & 2: He was silent,

READER 1: as a lamb about to be slaughtered

READER 2: and a sheep about to be sheared. *(from Isaiah 53:1-7)*

Solo: "Behold the Lamb" *(D. Rambo)*

READER 1: My God, my God, why have You deserted me?

READER 2: Why are You so far away?
You cannot help me or even hear me?

READER 1: O my God, I cry day and night,
but You do not hear me.
Anyone who sees me
laughs at me and mocks me, saying,

READER 2: "Since He trusted in the Lord to deliver Him,
let the Lord deliver Him."

READER 1: My body is decaying, my strength is leaving, I am dying.
Do not be far away from me, O Lord.

READERS 1 & 2: Come, help me, my strength. *(from Psalm 22)*

Solo: "At the Cross" *(Watts/Hudson, Verses 1 & 2)*

READERS 1 & 2: From noon until three o'clock
darkness covered the land.

READER 2: Then, at three, Jesus cried with a loud voice,

READER 1: "Eli, Eli, lama sabachthani?"

READER 2: That is to say,

READER 1: "My God, my God, why have You forsaken me?"

READERS 1 & 2: Jesus cried out again and died.

READER 2: Behold, the veil over the Holy of Holies
in the Temple in Jerusalem,
ripped in two from top to bottom.

READERS 1 & 2: There was an earthquake.

READER 1: Graves opened up to let out the bodies of dead believers

READER 2: who were seen around Jerusalem.

READER 1: When the centurion and those with him
witnessed all these things,

READERS 1 & 2: they were very much afraid.

READER 2: "Truly this was the Son of God," they said. *(from Matthew 27)*

Solo: "The Unveiled Christ" *(Herrell, Verse 1 & Chorus)*

READER 1: As the Sabbath ended

READER 2: and dawn broke on the first day of the week,

READER 1: some women,

READER 2: including Mary Magdalene, Mary, the mother of James, Joanna, and
Salome,

READERS 1 & 2: came to the tomb

READER 2: to place spices around Jesus' dead body.

READER 1: When they got there, they found the large stone,

READER 2: which had been placed at the mouth of the tomb,

READER 1: had been rolled back from the opening.

READER 2: The soldiers guarding the tomb were gone,
and an angel awaited them with a special message:

READER 1: "Do not be afraid,
I know you are looking for the crucified Jesus.
He is not here; He is alive, as He told you He would be!"
(from Matthew 28:1-7; Mark 16:1-7; Luke 24:1-10)

READER 2: Behold, how great God's love for us,
making it possible for us to become His children.

READER 1: The world does not recognize us,
because it did not recognize Him.

READERS 1 & 2: Beloved, we are God's children.

READER 1: One day, when He comes again,

READER 2: we will be like Him

READERS 1 & 2: and see Him in all His glory! *(from 1 John 1:1-3)*

Solo: "Our God Reigns" *(Smith)*

They Knew No Easter

by Sherry Schumann

Running Time: 1 hour

Cast:

NARRATOR—Reader for the introduction and closing

ROMAN SOLDIER—Soldier at the crucifixion who won Jesus' robe in a dice game

CENTURION—Centurion whose slave was healed by Jesus

JOSEPH OF ARIMATHEA—Member of the Sanhedrin who donates his burial tomb for Jesus

NICODEMUS—Pharisee and member of the Sanhedrin who assists Joseph of Arimathea in preparing Jesus' tomb

CAIAPHAS—Jewish high priest who accused Jesus of blasphemy

PONTIUS PILATE—Roman governor of Judea responsible for Jesus' crucifixion

BARABBAS—Criminal and zealot released from Roman custody instead of Jesus

MARY MAGDALENE—Devoted follower of Jesus

SALOME—Mother of James and John

JOHN THE BELOVED—One of the twelve disciples who was Jesus' closest friend

SIMON PETER—The disciple who denied Jesus three times

MARY—Jesus' mother

(Golgotha, small hill outside of Jerusalem at the foot of the cross; thirty minutes after Christ has died on the cross. Play opens with only a small light on the NARRATOR, *standing DS of the curtain.)*

NARRATOR: It was now about the sixth hour, and darkness came over the whole land until the ninth hour, for the sun stopped shining and the curtain of the Temple was torn in two. Jesus called out with a loud voice, "Father, into your hands I commit my spirit." When He had said this, He breathed His last . . .

(Pause for reflection)

> When all the people who had gathered to witness this sight saw what took place, they beat their breasts and went away. But all those who knew Him, including the women who had followed Him from Galilee, stood at a distance watching these things. (Luke 23:44-49)

(Light on NARRATOR *fades to black. Curtain rises on* ROMAN SOLDIER, *pensively standing at the foot of the cross.)*

ROMAN SOLDIER: I have seen hundreds crucified. It's gruesome business. One gets hardened; you have to or you don't survive. But it's no wonder that we Romans reserve death by crucifixion for only criminals and slaves.

Condemned prisoners are first stripped and scourged. The whip we use has rock and metal imbedded in it. Flogging the prisoners is the most humane thing I do because those who are bleeding die faster.

After the flogging they carry their own crossbars to the execution sites where the vertical poles are permanently installed. Then we drive nails through their wrists and ankles in order to anchor their bodies to the crosses. How do I do it? *(Shrugs)* It is just part of my job.

Death comes quickly for the lucky ones. Then we leave the bodies on the crosses until the vultures finish with them.

Today, we crucified three prisoners at Golgotha. Two of the prisoners were robbers. The third was convicted of treason. He had a charge nailed above His head. *"This is Jesus. The King of the Jews."* For some reason, that third prisoner got to me today. He was so badly beaten that we had to recruit an onlooker to carry the crossbar part of the way for Him. Yet, there was something about the look in His eyes. It was almost as if He knew something that we didn't know.

A small group of women, gathered at the foot of the cross, kept moaning His name over and over again. "Jesus, Jesus." A lot of other people seemed to enjoy hating Him. Even the robber hanging to His left sneered, "Are you the Christ? Then save yourself and save us!"

But the other robber, the one on the right, begged Him, "Jesus, remember me when You come into Your kingdom."

The King of the Jews said, "I tell you the truth, today you will be with me in paradise."

I don't know about any paradise. What I do know is that we crucified three prisoners today at Golgotha. Just another day on the job. I did get lucky, though. I won this robe throwing dice. *(Holds up robe)* It belonged to the King of the Jews!

But that look in His eyes . . . I don't know. Maybe it wasn't just another day after all.

*(*ROMAN SOLDIER *exits.* CENTURION *enters, incensed at the* ROMAN SOLDIER'S *speech.)*

CENTURION: It definitely was not "just another day." I saw Jesus look at the Roman soldiers throwing dice at the foot of the cross. And I heard Him gasp, "Father, forgive them for they know not what they do."

No, it was definitely not "just another day."

I knew Jesus. Last year, when I was living in Capernaum, my servant became ill. He had been devoted to me for years and I loved him like a member of my own family. I was frantic with grief at the thought of losing him. Then I heard about Jesus.

"Lord, do not trouble yourself," I said when I found the Rabbi teaching in the city, "for I do not deserve to have You come under my roof . . . I am a man under authority, with soldiers under me. I tell this one *go* and he goes, and this one *come* and he comes.   Just say the word and he will be healed."

Jesus said, "Never before have I found such great faith even in Israel." Immediately, my servant was healed.

No, today was no ordinary day. Jesus was crucified today . . . but under whose authority, I do not know.

He suffered for three hours, from noon until 3:00 P.M. During that time, darkness covered the land. Finally, in a loud voice, He called out, "Father, into Thy hands I commit my spirit." Then He breathed His last.

The earth shook under my feet, and I experienced fear unlike any I have ever known.

Surely, this was the Son of God.

(Long pause; looking out into the audience)

Why did He save my servant and not save himself?

*(*CENTURION *exits.* JOSEPH OF ARIMATHEA *and* NICODEMUS *enter the stage together.)*

NICODEMUS: We are both devout Jews and members of the Sanhedrin. For years now, we have both waited and searched for the Kingdom of God, a kingdom which I thought we had found . . . until today. Now that Jesus has died, what are we to believe, Joseph?

JOSEPH OF ARIMATHEA: Had you truly come to believe that Jesus was the Messiah, Nicodemus?

NICODEMUS: Yes, I had.

JOSEPH OF ARIMATHEA: I remember the night you were incredulous because Jesus said that one cannot see the Kingdom of God unless he is born again.

NICODEMUS: Yes. Jesus asked me how I could be one of Israel's teachers and not understand His words, but His words always came to me as riddles.

In fact, His life and now His death are nothing but a riddle to me. Jesus privately told me that the Son of Man had to be lifted up so that everyone who believes in Him will have eternal life. I believed that Jesus would be lifted up among men as the Son of Man. Instead, He was turned over to Roman authorities early this morning by our own Sanhedrin, severely beaten by Roman soldiers, and lifted upon a cross to die.

JOSEPH OF ARIMATHEA: You once quoted Jesus as saying, "Light has come into the world, but men love darkness instead of light because their deeds are evil." Nicodemus, I fear that today has been the darkest of all the days which the world has ever seen.

Our heathen masters will leave Jesus' body hanging on the cross for days and I cannot bear such a thought. Messiah or not, I love Him. I have a new tomb cut out of rock and can give Jesus a proper burial as the Law commands. Will you help me, my friend?

NICODEMUS: Of course. I have plenty of myrrh and spices available as we speak. Sundown is only a few hours away. We must hurry.

(They depart quickly. CAIAPHAS *enters dramatically as a powerful figure.)*

CAIAPHAS: Jesus of Nazareth. His claims were absurd . . . Lord of the Sabbath. Hah. Two eyewitnesses testified that He boasted about being able to destroy the Temple of God and rebuild it again in three days . . . a temple that took many men five hundred years to build. He even had the audacity to forgive sins. Only God can forgive sins.

Upon His arrest last night in the Garden of Gethsemane, I asked the Man directly, "Are you the Christ, the Son of God?" In my own presence, the lunatic claimed to be the Son of God.

A mere man who claims to be God? Our law requires that blasphemers be put to death. Jesus of Nazareth needed to die.

*(*CAIAPHAS *exits with a clear conscience.* PONTIUS PILATE *enters pensively, carrying a list.)*

PONTIUS PILATE: This morning at daybreak, the chief priests and entire Sanhedrin dragged Jesus of Nazareth into my courts. They handed me this list of crimes for which they wanted the Nazarene charged, accompanied by subtle threats that if these charges were thrown out, charges against me would be brought before Caesar for releasing a man who claimed to be a rival king.

Here is the list: inciting a rebellion, subverting a nation, opposing payment of taxes to Caesar, and claiming to be Christ, King of the Jews.

I found no basis for charging this man with a criminal act; in fact, He was no threat to Rome. I told the chief priests, "Take Him yourselves and judge Him by your own law."

"But we have no right to execute anyone," they replied.

"Execution," I thought. How could this Man be that great of a threat to the Sanhedrin?

I turned to Jesus and asked directly, "Are you the King of the Jews?"

He answered, "Yes. It is as you say." After that, Jesus refused to speak to me, except to say that I had no power over Him if it were not given to me from above.

Deranged? Maybe.

Delusional? Definitely.

Guilty? Definitely not.

I truly tried to set Him free. I knew about an old Jewish custom for the Roman governor to release one prisoner at the time of Passover. I asked the mob gathered outside, "Do you want me to release the King of the Jews?"

But they shouted, "No, not Him. Give us Barabbas!"

"Here is your King," I tried again.

The angry mob shouted, "Crucify Him! Crucify Him!"

"Shall I crucify your King?" I mocked . . . to which the chief priests and temple elders responded, "We have no king but Caesar."

(Turning to audience)

What would you have done?

The Jews have a custom of washing their hands as a way of disassociating oneself from a criminal act . . . As I washed my hands, I could not help but wonder, "Who is the criminal here—Jesus of Nazareth, the chief priests or . . . me?

*(*Pontius Pilate *exits, deep in thought.* Barabbas *enters with charisma.)*

Barabbas: Our people have suffered far too long under the tyranny and cruelty of Roman rule. I am Barabbas, condemned to die for standing up to the Romans. They call me a murderer, but I call myself a zealot.

Now this Jesus of Nazareth, He had the people "eating out of His hand." I heard that when He entered Jerusalem, they spread their cloaks on the ground. They shouted, "Blessed is He who comes in the name of the Lord!" The time *was* right! Jesus could have led a bloody rebellion against the Roman government and freed the nation of Israel, but He chose not to fight. Instead, in the face of death, He turned His cheek and the people of Israel turned their allegiance back towards me. Ironically, His silence paid the price for my freedom. But did Jesus' death on a cross buy freedom for anyone else?

*(*Barabbas *exits.* Mary Magdalene *rushes onto the stage as* Barabbas *exits.)*

Mary Magdalene: Freedom! What does Barabbas know about freedom? What does freedom for the nation of Israel really mean? Does freedom from the burden of Roman taxes or freedom from the crack of a Roman whip upon our backs guarantee the happiness of our nation? *(Emphatic)* No! *(Points to heart)* Freedom begins in here.

From the time that I was a young girl, I was a prisoner in my own body, tormented by demons. My life went from periods of crippling fear to violent rage—over which I had no control. The mental anguish, along with the physical pain, was at times unbearable. I knew no hope, no freedom from the torment . . . that is, until I met Jesus. His eyes penetrated deep within my soul—freeing me from the possession of seven demons and filling me with a warmth . . . a joy . . . a peace that I had never known.

My Jesus, my Rabboni, my Lord . . . He *was* the man destined to set the people free, but the people didn't know Him.

(MARY MAGDALENE *exits, crying.* SALOME *enters with a heavy heart.*)

SALOME: A mother has a responsibility to look out for the welfare of her children. My sons, James and John, are good men like their father, Zebedee. They worked in their father's fishing business until they met Jesus, and he called them to be disciples. Sure, Zebedee was hurt at first. After all, Zebedee is growing old and he had groomed his sons to one day take over the family business. But, Zebedee conceded that "a man has got to do what a man is called to do."

(Hands on hips)

Well, let me tell you, a mother has got to do what a mother has got to do . . . and that is to look out for the welfare of her children, even if they are nearly grown men! That is why I knelt before Jesus to ask him a favor. "What is it that you want?" asked Jesus.

I answered Him boldly, "Grant that one of these two sons of mine may sit at your right and the other at your left in your kingdom." After all, they had given up their positions in their father's business.

Jesus turned to my sons and asked, "Can you drink from the cup I am going to drink?" And my sons answered, "Yes."

When the other disciples heard about this they were indignant with my sons. Jesus called the twelve men together and said, ". . . whoever wants to become great among you must be your servant and whoever wants to be first must be your slave, just as the Son of Man did not come to be served, but to serve, and to give His life as a ransom for many."

Servants? Slaves? I told Zebedee that our sons would have been better off staying in the family business.

Last night as the Passover Feast was being served, Jesus got up from the table, took off his outer clothing, and wrapped a towel around his waist. After that, he poured water into a basin and began to wash the disciples' filthy feet, drying them with the towel that was wrapped around him.

Then Jesus said to them, "Now that I, your Lord and Teacher, have washed your feet, you also should wash one another's feet."

I've lived a long time, and I understand how the world works. I understand mothers who watch out for the welfare of their children. I understand sons who grow up to work in their fathers' businesses. I understand Rabbis who are called to teach. I can even understand that those who want to be great must at first be servants. But a Lord who washes his disciple's feet and a Lord who dies on the cross . . . *(Raising her hands as if to question God)* that, my God, I do not understand.

(SALOME *exits and the stage fades to black. The next scene interplays the thoughts of* JOHN THE BELOVED *and* SIMON PETER. JOHN THE BELOVED *enters the stage. A small light fades up on* SIMON PETER *who also remains onstage for the scene.*)

JOHN THE BELOVED: What are we going to do now? James, Andrew, Peter, me . . .

Three years ago we left our homes in Capernaum, deserted our boats along the shore, and devoted our lives to following Jesus. But now He is gone.

We were just simple fishermen, the four of us, until Jesus came. We were washing our nets after an unsuccessful night of fishing. A rather large crowd of people had gathered around the water's edge listening to the Teacher's words. With a quiet authority, Jesus climbed into Simon Peter's boat and asked him to put the boat out a little farther from the shore so that He could be better heard . . .

SIMON PETER: When Jesus finished speaking, He commanded me to put the boat into deep water and let down the nets for a catch. I didn't mean to be disrespectful, but I knew this Teacher didn't know a thing about fishing. I answered, "Master, we've worked hard all night and haven't caught a thing." Jesus just looked at me like He knew something that I didn't know. I nodded at Andrew to row us to one of the deep holes where we could let down our nets. Within minutes, the weight of the fish began to pull downward on the nets so much that some of the nets even began to rip!

I remember falling to my knees right there in the boat. Jesus simply lifted my chin and said, "Don't be afraid. Follow me, and I will make you fishers of men."

JOHN THE BELOVED: One evening we set across the Sea of Galilee towards Capernaum. A strong wind began to blow and the waters grew rough. We had rowed about three miles—halfway across the sea—when we saw Jesus approaching the boat. He was walking on the water. We were absolutely terrified. But Jesus called out, "It is I. Do not be afraid."

SIMON PETER: As Jesus walked towards us, I called out, "Jesus, if it is you, command me to come to you on the water."

"Come," He shouted over the roar of the wind.

I stepped out of the boat and began to walk towards Jesus. I was actually walking on the water! But then the winds grew stronger, and the waves drew my eyes away from the Master. I immediately began to sink. I remember screaming, "Lord, save me!"

Jesus stretched out His hand and caught me as a wave started to crash over my head. The storm was loud, but I could still hear His voice. "O you of little faith, why did you doubt?"

JOHN THE BELOVED: For three years we followed Him around the countryside listening to Him tell the crowds about the kingdom of God. On the way to Jerusalem, He pulled the twelve of us away from the crowds and tried to warn us. He said that He would be betrayed at the hands of the chief priests and would be condemned to die. I remember thinking that if the Master dies, I will die with Him. It never occurred to me that He would die and I would be left standing here all alone.

SIMON PETER: I always got so angry with His warnings and predictions. I could accept that kind of talk from Judas or the zealots or one of the others, but not Jesus. I called Him the Christ. I pledged my life to Him; He held my life in His hands.

I remember the first time Jesus tried to warn us. I took Him aside and tried to rebuke Him. Imagine me rebuking the One who successfully rebuked the Sea of Galilee. Anger flashed into His eyes when I told Him to stop talking about such things as betrayal and suffering and death. He said, "Get behind me, Satan. You do not have in mind the ways of God, but of man."

Last night was the worst of all. We were all gathered at the table in an upper room, a furnished guest room, outside the city. We were celebrating the Passover feast. Jesus quietly said that one of us would betray Him and that all of us would fall away. I told Him that I would never fall away. Jesus just looked at me—that same look He gave me when He hauled me up from the sea—and said, "I tell you the truth, before the rooster crows, you will disown me three times."

I told Him that even if I had to die with Him, I would never disown Him. Why did I always have to argue against His warnings?

Jesus was right, you know. I turned into a coward after He was arrested, afraid that the chief priests would arrest me too. I was warming my hands on a fire outside the high priest's courtyard. A servant girl asked me if I was one of the disciples, and I said, "No." Not once, not twice, but three times I denied the Master. I hope that I never again hear a rooster crow.

"Whoever wants to save his life will lose it, but whoever loses his life for me will save it." Jesus taught us that, and I believed Him. How could I have been such a complete coward, such a total fool? How could I have been so scared . . . *(choked with emotion)* so scared that I disowned my Lord?

(JOHN THE BELOVED *exits; light on* SIMON PETER *fades. Light fades up on* MARY, MOTHER OF JESUS, *sitting at the foot of the cross.*)

MARY, MOTHER OF JESUS: I held Him for years . . .

(Hands crossed over heart) I held Him in my heart after the angel of the Lord called out to me, "You will be with child and give birth to a son, and you are to call him Jesus."

(Hands holding stomach) I held Him in my womb as Elizabeth exclaimed, "Blessed are you among women and blessed is the child that you will bear!"

(Hands and arms cradling an imaginary baby) I held Him in my arms when He was presented at the Temple in Jerusalem and circumcised. It was there that both Simeon and Anna spoke about the redemption of Israel.

(Glancing down at her hands) Why could I not have held Him as He died?

(Looking upward) My God, Your ways are so hard . . .

(Looking at audience) A census mandated by Caesar Augustus had forced us to travel to Bethlehem during the last month of my pregnancy with Jesus. I rode our donkey while my husband walked alongside me. Joseph saw me grimace in pain as the first contraction gripped me. Taking the reins of the donkey away from my hands, Joseph reassured me that soon I would be resting in the most comfortable bed that Bethlehem had to offer. *(Pause)* Unfortunately, Bethlehem did not have a comfortable bed to offer; in fact, it had no bed at all. I soon realized that I was destined to give birth to my son in a lowly stable on the outskirts of town.

Panic and desperation filled Joseph's eyes as the contractions came upon me, one right after another. With a confidence that I did not have, I reassured Joseph.

"Remember, Joseph, God is with us. Please go now quickly and tell the innkeeper's wife that my time has come." Hours later, Jesus' first cry pierced the night air and Joseph wept to behold God's Son.

(Long pause to reflect; looking up to God)

Do you remember the sheer terror that seized me when I thought that Jesus was lost? We were traveling home from Jerusalem after celebrating the Feast of the Passover. It was an exciting time for Joseph and me, because at the age of 12, Jesus was finally able to join us for the celebration. Little did I know that this trip would mark Jesus' transition from a boy to a man. For safety in numbers, we traveled in a large caravan consisting of extended family and friends from our home town of Nazareth. During the trip to Jerusalem, Jesus traveled in the rear of the caravan with His cousins and His friends.

I wasn't concerned when we did not see Him throughout the first morning of our journey home. However, when Jesus had not appeared by late afternoon, I began to look for Him among our company of travelers. A terrifying realization soon dawned that no one had seen Jesus the entire day.

Two horrible days elapsed as Joseph and I retraced our steps to Jerusalem and finally found Jesus calmly discussing the Law with the teachers at the Temple courts. The terror that had gripped me during our two day search quickly flamed into anger. "Son, why have you treated us like this?" I demanded, "Your father and I have been anxiously searching for you."

Jesus was confused by my question and asked, "Why were you looking for me? Didn't you know I had to be in my Father's house?" His Father's house. I understood then that the four stone walls of our modest house in Nazareth would never again be my son's home.

(Long pause to reflect)

Jesus' brothers and I went to hear Jesus speak early in His ministry. Word quickly passed that we had arrived. The crowd that was sitting around Jesus said, "Your mother and brothers are outside looking for you."

I understood the message that He was trying to convey, but it still broke my heart to hear Jesus reply, "Who is my mother? Who are my brothers? . . . Whoever does God's will is my brother and sister and mother."

(Long pause)

Today was just too much for any mother to bear. Simeon had told me, "A sword will pierce your soul too." He was right.

(Long pause; crying as she looks up to God)

From the first time that I held Him, I understood that Jesus was Yours, and I gave Him to You . . . My God, why couldn't I have just held Him as He died?

(MARY crumbles onstage, prostrated before the cross, crying. Lights fade to black. Light fades up on NARRATOR.)

NARRATOR *(addressing the audience):* With whom do you most identify?

• The Soldier . . . who won a robe and admitted that Good Friday might not be just another day.

- Caiaphas . . . who believed that Jesus was a blasphemer and deserved to die.
- The Centurion . . . who questioned under whose authority Jesus was put to death.
- Mary Magdalene . . . who, in knowing Jesus as the Son of God, experienced freedom from inner torment.
- Peter . . . who denied His Lord.

Or do you identify with one of the others?

At the ninth hour on that Good Friday afternoon more than two thousand years ago Jesus said, "It is finished."

The witnesses knew no Easter that afternoon. They knew only that Jesus . . . was dead.

Blackout

Production Note: Blackout may signal either a transition or the end of the performance. An a cappella solo would be appropriate here, followed by a final monologue by Mary Magdalene entitled, *Called by Name*. If this is the end of a Palm Sunday or Good Friday performance, it is imperative that the program requests the audience to leave in silence and extends an invitation to join the congregation for the conclusion, *Called by Name*, during the Easter morning worship service.

Called by Name

by Sherry Schumann

Running Time: 5 to 10 minutes

Cast:

MARY MAGDALENE—Devoted friend and follower of Jesus

(Jerusalem, years after Jesus' crucifixion and resurrection.)

MARY MAGDALENE: On that first glorious Easter morning, my Savior greeted me by my name.

I remember so well the devastation and despair that we all experienced the Friday afternoon that Jesus died. Had we been wrong? Had Jesus deceived us? Had we mistaken a mere man to be the Messiah?

But beneath my despair, I clung desperately to a tiny flicker of hope. I had to believe. You may remember that I had once traveled a life of hopelessness, tormented by seven demons. But Jesus was the one who had freed me and filled me with peace.

As I looked upon His lifeless body on the cross, my heart cried out, "If you do not live, my Lord, then how can I?"

We watched as Joseph of Arimathea and Nicodemus quickly removed His body and carried it to a tomb. They wrapped His body in strips of linen, alternating with a mixture of myrrh and aloes, in accordance with our burial customs. The setting sun signaled the Shabbat Shalom, our greeting for the Sabbath. The men placed His body in the tomb sealed behind a huge stone. It was understood that we women would return after the Sabbath to complete preparations for the burial.

Early Sunday morning, I accompanied Mary, mother of Jesus, and Salome to the tomb. We were laden with grief. We made an effort to focus our thoughts on the practical side of burial: "Did we have enough spices?" and "How are we going to move the stone when we get there?"

My eyes were cast down as we approached the tomb. Then I heard Mary gasp. I looked up. Our worst fears had come true. Someone had rolled the stone away and broken into the Master's tomb. How much more grief would we have to endure? Immediately, the three of us began to run, retracing our steps back to the city. Being younger than Mary or Salome, I reached the disciples first. "They have taken the Lord out of the tomb, and we do not know where they have put Him!" I cried.

My own steps were no match for Peter and John's strides as they ran towards the burial site of our Teacher. I could not keep up, but arrived after they had entered the tomb. Finding the tomb empty—the linen strips and burial cloth neatly folded—Peter and John returned home.

I lingered outside the tomb; the depth of my sorrow and grief knew no bounds. That tiny flicker of hope which I had held onto so desperately since Friday had begun to fade. Tears began to stream down my face. I stooped to look back in the empty tomb, and there were two angels in white, sitting where Jesus' body had lain, one at the head and on at the feet! They asked me why I was weeping and I said, "Because they have taken away my Lord, and I don't know where they have laid Him." I turned around and it was then that I saw the gardener. He asked, "Woman, why are you crying? Who are you looking for?"

Responding to him, I said, "Sir, if you have taken my Lord, tell me where you put Him!"

Then I heard His voice speak my name, "Mary." And I recognized—not the gardener—but my Lord. "Rabboni," I cried as I fell at His feet to worship Him. My joy exceeded all bounds. That tiny flicker of hope, nearly quenched by the devastation of His crucifixion and then again by His empty tomb, erupted into a flame within my soul. All doubt, all devastation, all lost hope was gone when I heard my Lord call my name.

My Jesus, my Lord, my Savior and Messiah had victoriously conquered death and now lived!

(Long pause)

It has been years now since that glorious Easter morning. Today and every day, the flame burns brightly in my soul. And when I close my eyes, I can still hear my Savior call my name.

(MARY MAGDALENE *exits with joy and hope.)*